CONTENTS

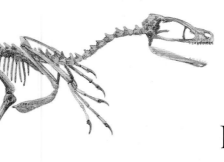

Some words are printed in bold, **like this**. You can find out what they mean in the glossary.

EXTINCTION IS FOREVER

Everyone knows that dinosaurs became extinct millions of years ago, but what is extinction? Extinction occurs when the last representative of a species dies. It takes place if a species fails to adapt to changing conditions in its environment or has lost out to superior competition. Most species remain on Earth for no more than 10 million years, so to some extent extinction is inevitable. At least 99.9 percent of all the plants and animals that ever lived on Earth are extinct. The average lifespan for a species is five to seven million years. Exceptions are the so-called "living fossils" that survive with very few obvious changes for many millions of years.

Background or mass extinction?

During the four billion years of the history of life on Earth, the rate of extinction has generally been slow. During the past 542 million years of the **Phanerozoic** eon the **background extinction** rate has been two to four families of living things every million years. In contrast to this slow but steady turnover are sudden mass extinctions. This is when huge numbers of organisms go extinct in a relatively short period of time. In one major extinction event, roughly 251 million years ago, all life was threatened and most species disappeared. In another event, around 65.95 million years ago,

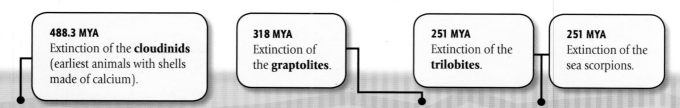

488.3 MYA
Extinction of the **cloudinids** (earliest animals with shells made of calcium).

318 MYA
Extinction of the **graptolites**.

251 MYA
Extinction of the **trilobites**.

251 MYA
Extinction of the sea scorpions.

500 MYA

400 MYA

300 MYA

MYA = million years ago

EXTINCTIONS
OF
LIVING THINGS

MICHAEL BRIGHT

Heinemann
LIBRARY

www.heinemannlibrary.co.uk
Visit our website to find out more information about Heinemann Library books.

To order:
☎ Phone +44 (0) 1865 888066
▤ Fax +44 (0) 1865 314091
▥ Visit www.heinemannlibrary.co.uk

Heinemann Library is an imprint of Capstone Global Library Limited, a company incorporated in England and Wales having its registered office at 7 Pilgrim Street, London, EC4V 6LB – Registered company number: 6695582

"Heinemann" is a registered trademark of Pearson Education Limited, under licence to Capstone Global Library Limited.

Text © Capstone Global Library Limited 2009
First published in hardback in 2009
Paperback edition first published in 2010
The moral rights of the proprietor have been asserted.

Edited by Pollyanna Poulter
Designed by Steven Mead and Q2A Creative Solutions
Original illustrations © Pearson Education Limited by International Mapping and Stuart Jackson-Carter/ The Art Agency
Picture research by Elizabeth Alexander
Production by Alison Parsons
Originated by Dot Gradations
Printed in China by Leo Paper Group

ISBN 978 0 431064 72 7 (hardback)
13 12 11 10 09
10 9 8 7 6 5 4 3 2 1

ISBN 978 0 431064 78 9 (paperback)
14 13 12 11 10
10 9 8 7 6 5 4 3 2 1

British Library Cataloguing-in-Publication Data
Bright, Michael
 Extinctions of living things. - (Timeline : life on Earth)
 1. Extinction (Biology) - Juvenile literature
 I. Title
 576.8'4
A full catalogue record for this book is available from the British Library.

Acknowledgments

We would like to thank the following for permission to reproduce photographs: © Alamy: pp. 21 (E.R. Degginger), 37 (yogesh more); © ardea.com: p. 30 (Ian Beames); © Audubon Nature Institute, New Orleans: p. 45; © Corbis: pp. 19 (Sanford/Agliolo), 36 (Rickey Rogers/Reuters), 42 (Layne Kennedy), 43 (Sergei Cherkashin/Reuters), 44 (Ted Horowitz); © Department of the Interior: p. 20 (USGS); © Getty Images: pp. 14 (National Geographic), 33 (Time & Life Pictures); © imagequestmarine.com: pp. 13 (Kelvin Aitken/V&W), 31 (Kike Calvo/V&W), 39 (Mark Conlin/V&W); © Istockphoto: pp. 4, 16, 26, 32 and **40 chapter openers**, and **all panel backgrounds** (duuuna), 12 (Henry Chaplin); © John Game: p. 46; © NHMPL: p. 22 (Michael Long); © Photolibrary: pp. 7 (OSF/Jim Gathany), 31 and 35 (OSF/Michael Fogden), 41 (OSF/Juniors Bildarchiv); © Science Photo Library: pp. 5 (Richard T. Nowitz), 15 (Peter Scoones), 23 (Christian Darkin), 25 (NASA), 27 (Photo Researchers), 28 (Chris Butler); © The Manitoba Museum: p. 24; © The Natural History Museum, London: p. 6.

Cover photograph of carnivorous dinosaur fossil reproduced with permission of © Mehau Kulyk (Science Photo Library), and Earth from space © NASA.

We would like to thank Prof. Norman MacLeod and Gavin Fidler for their invaluable help in the preparation of this book.

Every effort has been made to contact copyright holders of material reproduced in this book. Any omissions will be rectified in subsequent printings if notice is given to the Publishers.

Disclaimer
All the Internet addresses (URLs) given in this book were valid at the time of going to press. However, due to the dynamic nature of the Internet, some addresses may have changed, or sites may have changed or ceased to exist since publication. While the author and Publishers regret any inconvenience this may cause readers, no responsibility for any such changes can be accepted by either the author or the Publishers.

The mosasaur was one of the first animals to be described as extinct. Mosasaurs were marine reptiles that dominated the seas 95–65 million years ago.

all dinosaurs except the birds became extinct. Scientists have now proven that birds are dinosaur descendants (see page 11).

Human influence

About 100,000 years ago, the natural order on Earth changed – modern people arrived. Since then the level of extinction has risen dramatically. Biologist E. O. Wilson, of Harvard University, USA, has predicted that if the planet continues to be damaged by human activity, one half of all species on Earth will be extinct just 100 years from now. This would be a mass extinction caused entirely by humans.

EXTINCTION RECOGNIZED

Until the late 18th century it was widely believed that every living thing was created once and was there for all time. However, in the mid-1770s, the huge skull of an unknown creature was found in a mine next to the River Meuse in the Netherlands. It was later moved to a museum in Paris where French naturalist Georges Cuvier (see page 6) studied it. He rightly suggested that it was a monster marine reptile, now known as a **mosasaur.** His contemporaries suggested that it came from a creature "hiding" in a remote part of the world but Cuvier described it as a "creature hard to hide", even in the vast ocean. He believed that it must have disappeared from the face of the Earth. This is one of the first documented examples of a natural extinction.

199.6 MYA
Extinction of the **conodonts**.

65.95 MYA
Extinction of the **ammonites** and non-avian dinosaurs.

| 200 MYA | 100 MYA | 1 MYA | Present day |

GEORGES CUVIER
(1769–1832)

Georges Cuvier was one of the most influential scientists of his time. He was the first to persuade his fellow biologists that a way of explaining fossils is that plants and animals become extinct.

While others expected to find mammoths living in the unexplored western part of North America, and thought that dinosaur bones came from giants, Cuvier was explaining the differences between extinct animals by examining little more than their teeth. He was so skilled that it is said he could reconstruct an entire skeleton from a single fossil bone!

Cuvier was responsible for building the first reconstruction of a giant sloth (*Megatherium*). His work is considered to be the foundation of the study of fossil animals with backbones – modern **vertebrate** palaeontology.

Cuvier died before Charles Darwin proposed his theory of evolution in 1859, so he knew nothing of the Englishman's revolutionary ideas about evolution. Indeed, Cuvier believed that the number and type of species was fixed and did not evolve through time. He did, however, suggest that the past history of life could be explained by catastrophic events causing the sudden extinction of many living things. It was a view revisited in modern studies of mass extinctions and is now thought to be exactly what happened.

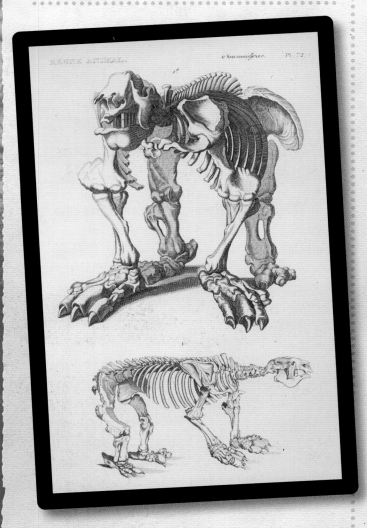

▲ *Engravings of the South American giant ground sloth* Megatherium. *It lived 2 million–8,000 years ago and was the size of an elephant.*

Planned extinctions

There are some organisms, especially bacteria and disease-causing viruses, that people would like to remove from the world. These eradication programmes are called "planned extinctions". As part of a successful planned extinction, the infectious disease smallpox has been eliminated in the wild since 1979. Similarly, polio and guinea worm disease are close to being eliminated. At one time, guinea worm disease infected 3.5 million people in 20 countries. It is a painful, disfiguring disease caused by a parasitic worm that grows up to one metre long inside its human host. An eradication programme started in the early 1980s has had considerable success. In 2005, there were fewer than 10,000 cases in nine countries, and the World Health Organization (WHO) believes that the disease is close to disappearing altogether.

Malaria – going, going, gone

In 2003, biologist Olivia Judson, of Imperial College in London, UK, proposed that a planned extinction could be used to wipe out malaria from the tropics. The plan would be to breed mosquitoes carrying **genes** that make them infertile and release them into the wild. Malaria-carrying mosquitoes would then mate with these infertile insects, so the species would fail to reproduce and eventually die out. There are, she argues, just 30 species out of 2,700 species of mosquitoes that carry the malaria **parasite**. These represent only one percent of mosquito species and their removal is unlikely to upset any ecosystem. More than 300 million people in developing countries could benefit from what Judson has called "the ultimate swatting".

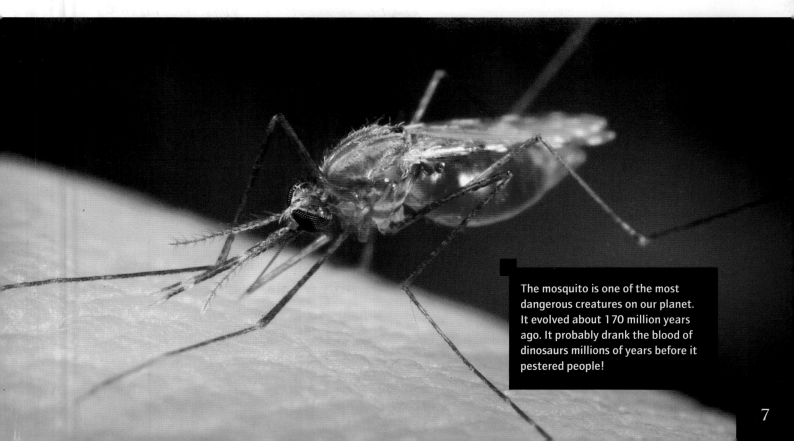

The mosquito is one of the most dangerous creatures on our planet. It evolved about 170 million years ago. It probably drank the blood of dinosaurs millions of years before it pestered people!

Going together: co-extinctions

When a parasite's host becomes extinct, the parasite is likely to become extinct, too. If a plant loses the animal that pollinates its flowers, such as the fig wasp and fig, it also might become extinct. Similarly, if prey disappears so might the **predator**. For example, in New Zealand the local Maori people killed off the giant ostrich-like moa. Its main predator, Haast's eagle – the largest eagle ever to have lived – disappeared as well. This is called **co-extinction**.

Haast's eagle was the principle predator of New Zealand's flightless moa, but when the moa became extinct the eagle disappeared too.

Flower's demise

In the Hawaiian Islands the extinction of several species of birds almost led to the extinction of the mountain hibiscus. Rats that came with early settlers had already eaten and destroyed the hibiscus's seeds. Then, with European settlers, came cats, mosquitoes, and bird flu. These wiped out several species of honeycreeper, a bird that pollinated hibiscus flowers. Three out of seven species of the mountain hibiscus then became extinct.

Reprieve

When the passenger pigeon became extinct in 1914 (see page 30), most of its parasites also went extinct. Scientists believed that this included the parasitic flight-feather louse, *Columbicola extincta*. They thought this was a classic case of co-extinction, but in 2000 the louse was rediscovered alive and well. It was living on band-tailed pigeons, the largest species of pigeon in North America. The louse was not extinct after all. This case drew attention to the fact that for every large animal extinction there might be many more species, such as lice, mites, and other small parasites that are lost with them.

Local extinctions

Co-extinction, like all extinctions, can occur on a local as well as a global level. The species becomes locally extinct but still survives elsewhere in the world. In the south of England, for example, the large blue butterfly is dependent on a species of red ant that looks after its caterpillar. When **myxomatosis** killed many rabbits in the 1950s, the grass grew and the habitat became less attractive to red ants, so there were fewer ant nests. This led to the large blue butterfly becoming extinct in many areas. However, when rabbit populations recovered and the grass was cropped once more, the red ants returned. Conservationists were able to reintroduce the large blue butterfly to places where it was once abundant.

PARASITES AND HOSTS

Parasites are organisms that live on or inside another organism and do it harm. The organism that has been invaded is called the host. Many parasites have specific hosts and some have more than one host during their life cycle. In one type of host, called the **"definitive host"**, the parasite reproduces sexually, while in the **"intermediate host"** it does not reproduce sexually, but can reproduce asexually. For example, the broad fish tapeworm's intermediate host is a fish while its definitive host is a mammal. Similarly, the common liver fluke has an aquatic snail as its intermediate host, while cattle, sheep, and occasionally humans are its definitive host. Both definitive and intermediate host need to be present in order for the parasites to complete their life cycle. If one host should become extinct then the parasite becomes extinct, too.

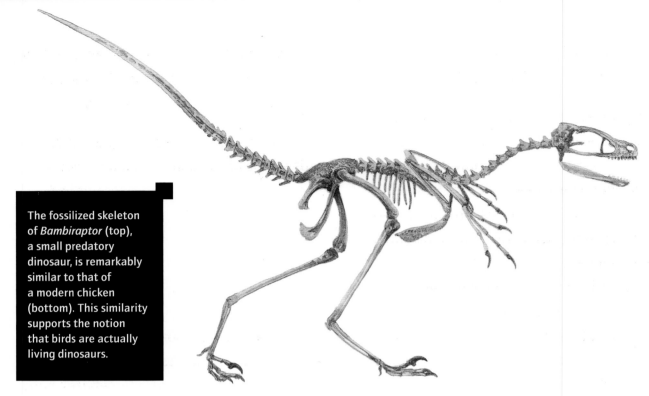

The fossilized skeleton of *Bambiraptor* (top), a small predatory dinosaur, is remarkably similar to that of a modern chicken (bottom). This similarity supports the notion that birds are actually living dinosaurs.

False extinctions

Rather than disappearing altogether, an organism might evolve into something else that continues the line. This process is known as "**pseudo-extinction**". It is a natural turnover of generations in which parent species die out and daughter species remain alive. As a living species must have had an ancestral species from which it evolved, it could be that much of evolution is the result of pseudo-extinction. Examples exist, but its relative frequency is unknown and it is difficult to prove. For example, the horse-like Eohippus is thought to be pseudo-extinct. All subsequent horse species are considered daughter species of Eohippus. But it has yet to be proved they had a common ancestor.

Dinosaurs alive and well

When the great dinosaurs disappeared 65 million years ago, many mammal species went extinct too. However, about 40 percent of these were thought to be pseudo-extinctions where the daughter species of these mammals changed to fill many of the niches left by the dinosaurs. This process is known as "**adaptive radiation**". It gave rise to the mammal species we see today.

The process of pseudo-extinction might also be true of the dinosaurs themselves.

It is generally believed that some dinosaur species are actually pseudo-extinct and that modern birds are their daughter species. This is not a new idea. As far back as the 19th century, Darwin's close friend Thomas Henry Huxley (1825–1895) drew attention to the similarity of birds and reptiles. However, it was not until about 1969 that palaeontologist John H. Ostrom (1928–2005) identified similarities between the dinosaur *Deinonychus,* sometimes depicted as a feathered dinosaur, and the first known bird, *Archaeopteryx*. In 1986, Jacques A.

Gauthier of Yale University, USA, analysed the evidence and constructed a family tree that grouped the birds firmly with dinosaurs.

For some time scientists have suggested that birds are the descendants of a **maniraptoran** dinosaur. These fast-running dinosaurs had modified wrist bones that provided a grasping ability for the dinosaur, but would also have made flight possible for birds. This transition from dinosaurs to birds is believed to have taken place in the Jurassic period, about 150 million years ago. In 2008, research on protein retrieved from a *Tyrannosaurus rex* provided the first firm evidence of the link between birds and dinosaurs.

Birds are the daughter species of pseudo-extinct dinosaur species, and one bird kept the "terrible lizard" tradition alive. It was the terror bird, a voracious predator of ancient horses that took the place of *Tyrannosaurus rex* to become one of the world's top predators.

Cross-sections of fossil ammonites and nautiloids, which lived 400–65 million years ago, show chambered shells similar to those of the modern pearly nautilus. The pearly nautilus has changed very little from nautiloids that lived 300 million years ago, so we consider it a "living fossil".

Living fossils

Many species face changes to their environment that they cannot adapt to, making them obsolete. However, some species are so in tune with their environment that they appear to have changed very little for millions of years. "Living fossil" is a term sometimes used to describe these species. They closely resemble, but are not necessarily the same as, fossils found in rocks thousands or even millions of years old. Our seas and rivers hide several living fossils.

Swimming fossils

The chambered nautilus is a living relative of octopuses and squid. It looks like creatures that lived 500 million years ago and were closely related to the ammonites. Another "living fossil", the eel-like frilled shark, is found at depths of over 1,000 m (3,300 ft.) in all the world's oceans. It has six frilly, collar-like gill slits and teeth with three cusps – both primitive features. Its teeth are like those of shark fossils found in the rocks of the **Pliocene** (5.33–2.59 million years ago) in Europe and the **Miocene** (23.03–5.33 million years ago) in the Caribbean.

In the rivers of eastern North America there are two bony fishes that have changed little since the dinosaurs roamed the Earth – the bowfin and the alligator gar. Their extinct Jurassic relative *Leedsicthys* is the largest fish ever known to have lived. Fossils from Peterborough, England, indicate that it was 18–22 m (60–72 ft.) long. The living alligator gar is much smaller but still an impressive fish at 3 m (10 ft.) long. The bowfin is just 1 m (3.3 ft.) long.

Living fossil plants

The ginkgo or maidenhair tree is recognised by its unusual fan-shaped leaves. It has no close living relatives, but fossils of ginkgo leaves have been found in **Permian** rocks that are 270 million years old. Today, the tree is cultivated in gardens and parks all over the world, but it is found in the wild in only two areas of Zhejiang Province in eastern China.

Frilled sharks were thought to be extinct until one was caught in the deep sea off Japan in the 18th century. They grow up to 2 m (6.5 ft.) long and have primitive features.

FOSSIL FUEL FOOD

Spring in Delaware Bay on the US east coast is marked by the arrival of millions of shorebirds. They stop here to rest and refuel on their migration to breeding sites in the Arctic. Their fuel comes from the sea. At this time, thousands of horseshoe crabs emerge from the ocean to deposit their eggs in the sand. These strange and primitive-looking creatures are actually marine relatives of spiders. They probably descended from sea scorpions that lived 500 million years ago, and have changed very little in the past 300 million years. Today, the birds eat the horseshoe crab eggs, but little do they know that they are consuming the offspring of a "living fossil".

Lazarus species

When examining fossils, scientists sometimes find that species disappear from the rocks, only to reappear millions of years later, either as more recent fossils or as living species. These are known as "**Lazarus species**" rather than "living fossils". They are named after a man in a Bible story who was thought to have been raised from the dead. David Jablonski, of the University of Chicago, USA, first coined this term.

A classic example of a Lazarus species is the **coelacanth**. This modern creature represents a group of fish thought to have become extinct between 70 and 80 million years ago.

Laughing gulls feast on the eggs of horseshoe crabs. The crabs emerge from the sea to deposit their eggs in the sand. Horseshoe crabs have kept the same body plan for over 300 million years.

Coelacanths are related to lungfishes and early amphibians. They have lobe-shaped fins that were the forerunners of amphibian limbs. Today, they live and hunt in deep water and rest in submarine caves.

Today, two species of coelacanth live in deep waters around the western rim of the Indian Ocean, and off the Indonesian island of Sulawesi. Their nearest relatives are found in rocks from the **Cretaceous** period, when dinosaurs dominated the Earth. No fossils of coelacanths have been found in rocks younger than 70–80 million years old. So it came as a big surprise when a coelacanth, plucked freshly from the sea, was found in a South African fish market in 1938. Since then, living coelacanths have been found and filmed in deep waters off the Comoro Islands, Madagascar, South Africa, East Africa, and Indonesia.

More surprises

The Laotian rock rat was another big surprise. In 1996, it was found in a local meat market in Thakhek, Laos. The remains of three more were discovered in the pellets regurgitated by owls that must have eaten them. At first the rat was thought to represent a new family of mammals. However, it was later recognised as being from a family of bushy-tailed rodents. Scientists had previously only seen these as 11 million year old fossils. Some Lazarus examples are even smaller. A rare ant called *Gracilidris* was known only from a specimen trapped in a piece of amber 15–20 million years old. In Paraguay in 2006, US and Argentine researchers, Alex Wild and Fabiana Cuezzo, accidentally found long-legged ants that walked in a strangely upright manner and matched the ant in the fossil. *Gracilidris* was most definitely alive and well.

With no fossil evidence it is difficult to explain why species should disappear and reappear. A simple explanation is that an extinction event caused the population to drop but didn't make it extinct. Fossils would therefore be rare. It could be that they exist somewhere in the rocks, but have yet to be found.

MASS
EXTINCTIONS

Throughout Earth's history there have been several sudden catastrophic events resulting in the extinction of huge numbers of plant and animal species. Some took place over a relatively short geological period of time (perhaps no more than tens of thousands of years), some over several million years. Palaeontologists study fossils and recognise these events – in one layer of sedimentary rock, plant and animal fossils are present; in the layer above, they are not. Mass extinctions usually involve a broad range of species, from the simplest, such as **algae** and bacteria, to the most complex, such as reptiles and mammals.

The most well known extinction event occurred roughly 65 million years ago. This was when the dinosaurs and their relatives, such as the pterosaurs, **mosasaurs**, and plesiosaurs, were wiped out. But that was only one of many extinction events. By examining the occurrence and absence of fossils in rocks, scientists now know that mass extinctions have occurred many times since life appeared on our planet. In 1982, two palaeontologists from the University of Chicago, USA (David Raup and Jack Sepkoski) identified five major extinction events. These are known as the "Big Five" and are listed in the table opposite.

488.3 MYA
Cambrian-Ordovician extinction.

443.7 MYA
Ordovician-Silurian extinction.

359.2 MYA
Late Devonian extinction.

251 MYA
Permian-Triassic extinction.

| 500 MYA | 400 MYA | 300 MYA |

MYA = million years ago

Taking over

Major mass extinctions and the continuing **background extinctions** between them have had a huge effect on evolution, enabling it to accelerate. It is not necessarily that superior species took over. The once dominant species were eliminated and replaced by new species. At the end of the **Cretaceous**, for example, mammals were small and unable to compete with the powerful dinosaurs. They had their opportunity for greatness when the dinosaurs disappeared, but powerful birds, such as the terror bird (see page 11), the daughter species of dinosaurs, took over instead. It was not until this second dominant "dinosaur" **fauna** was eliminated, during a period of cooling across the planet, that the mammals underwent a period of rapid evolution and many new species appeared. Some mammal species, such as mammoths, mastodons, and elephants, evolved into species almost the size of the largest dinosaurs!

THE "BIG FIVE"

Extinction event	Approx. mya	Impact
Ordovician-Silurian	443.7	Second largest event, took place over 3 million years with 85 percent of marine species becoming extinct, including species of brachiopods, bryozoans, **trilobites**, conodonts, and graptolites.
Late **Devonian**	359.2	A series of extinctions that took place over more than 3 million years. Removed 70 percent of all known species, mostly marine and including the jawless fishes. Freshwater species were less affected.
Permian-**Triassic** or the 'Great Dying'	251	Largest extinction event, eliminated 90 to 95 percent of marine species and 70 percent of land species, including some species of plants and the mammal-like reptiles.
Triassic-Jurassic	199.6	Event happened in less than 10,000 years, knocking out 50 percent of known species, including the large **amphibians**. With these gone it paved the way for the rise of the dinosaurs.
Cretaceous-**Tertiary**	65.95	About 50 percent of known species disappeared, including the dinosaurs, mosasaurs, plesiosaurs, pterosaurs, as well as many plants and invertebrates. The early birds and mammals survived this event.

199.6 MYA
Triassic-Jurassic extinction.

65.95 MYA
Cretaceous-Tertiary extinction.

PRESENT DAY
Holocene extinction.

EXTINCTION INTENSITY

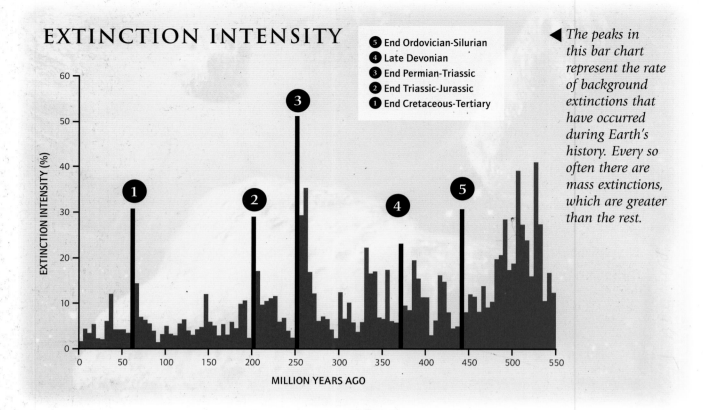

5 End Ordovician-Silurian
4 Late Devonian
3 End Permian-Triassic
2 End Triassic-Jurassic
1 End Cretaceous-Tertiary

◀ *The peaks in this bar chart represent the rate of background extinctions that have occurred during Earth's history. Every so often there are mass extinctions, which are greater than the rest.*

It came from outer space

The cause of mass extinctions is very difficult to pin down. Older rocks contain fewer fossils so less evidence is available. Therefore, scientists can only suggest theories about mass extinction causes. All are highly debated and include:

- major volcanic activity;
- global warming or cooling;
- major changes in sea level;
- changes in atmospheric composition;
- release of noxious chemicals in the sea;
- plate tectonics;
- exploding stars;
- impact from extraterrestrial bodies.

26-million-year-cycle

David Raup and Jack Sepkoski analyzed data relating to the fate of marine creatures over the past 250 million years. Their research revealed a pattern of mass extinction events. They suggest that, since the end of the Permian, these events have taken place roughly every 26 million years. Two events – at the end of the Cretaceous and in the late **Eocene** – coincide with known meteorite impacts.

Raup and Sepkoski suggest all mass extinctions could be linked to regularly occurring collisions with asteroids, meteorites, or comets. From time to time, for example, our solar system crosses paths with the **Oort comet cloud**. This could send comets slamming into Earth for several million years. Many researchers have denied this idea. However, some think the suggestion credible, proposing that impacts are related to the behaviour of a companion star to the Sun, known as Nemesis. As yet Nemesis has still to be found.

Impact craters on the Earth's surface are evidence that large objects from space occasionally hit our planet. Some of those impacts coincide with mass extinction events.

Cosmic sources

Destructive radiation from outside the solar system is another possible cause. NASA acknowledges that a burst of **gamma rays,** shot from an exploding star within 6,000 **light years**, could be strong enough to strip away half of Earth's **ozone layer**. This would allow lethal **ultraviolet radiation** to penetrate Earth's atmosphere. It may interact with atmospheric molecules to create a super-aurora – a bright flash would fry anything not in the shade and turn the atmosphere into an oven for many weeks. Unfortunately, gamma rays leave no traces in the rocks so this theory is difficult to prove.

Another cosmic theory comes from Hans Jörg Fahr, University of Bonn, Germany. Our solar system orbits the centre of the Milky Way every 250 million years, passing through dense clouds of **interstellar matter** every 60 million years. The **solar wind** normally acts like a shield to protect Earth but at these times it is overwhelmed by the sudden influx of particles. They spill into the atmosphere, smash into air molecules and the fragments attract droplets of water to form clouds. The result is exceptionally dense cloud cover, a severe drop in global temperature, and the prospect of a damp and dark planet.

Theories of extraterrestrial bombardment, if true, would mean evolution is shaped by external forces, not just events on Earth. Bodies from space colliding with our planet is not rare, but what kind of impact they had on the history of life on Earth is still far from clear.

What killed the dinosaurs?

The non-avian dinosaurs disappeared at the end of the Cretaceous period, about 65.95 million years ago. Whether it was sudden or gradual is difficult to assess, but rocks below the Cretaceous-Tertiary boundary (K/T boundary) have dinosaur fossils and those above do not. Many reasons have been given for their demise, including:

- mammals eating dinosaur eggs;
- acid rain from volcanoes;
- diseases ravaging dinosaur populations;
- the impact of an asteroid.

Dinosaurs were not the only casualties. Life in the oceans was hit hard, from microscopic forms, such as **plankton**, right through to **ammonites** and marine reptiles. Outside the oceans, the last of the pterosaurs fell out of the sky, and plant communities worldwide were disrupted.

Iridium and a crater

The theory that an asteroid hitting Earth killed the dinosaurs became a credible explanation in 1980. Luis and Walter Alvarez of the University of California at Berkeley, USA, announced that they had found an **iridium**-rich layer within rocks in Italy, Denmark, and New Zealand. It coincided with the K/T boundary. Iridium is a rare element on our planet's surface, but it is abundant in meteorites, so an extraterrestrial cause could not be ruled out.

This theory was given another boost when geologists discovered an impact crater at Mexico's Yucatan Peninsula. The crater is 180 km (112 miles) wide and was made by an asteroid, about 10 km (6.2 miles) in diameter, hitting Earth roughly 65 million years ago. The initial explosion threw enormous quantities of dust into the atmosphere.

This picture is based on a satellite image. It shows the Manicouagan impact crater in Canada, which was caused by a 5 km (3 mile) diameter asteroid. The crater was 100 km (62 miles) across and is 215 million years old.

Earth would have roasted momentarily then cooled, causing extreme global climatic changes. All this seems to point to an extraterrestrial origin, but there were other dramatic changes taking place at the same time.

Volcanoes

Towards the end of the Cretaceous, volcanic activity increased on Earth. In India, episodic, widespread eruptions spewed out floods of lava and threw dust and sulfur **aerosols** into the air. This might have blocked out the Sun and reduced photosynthesis in plants. These eruptions took place during a time period of 800,000 years, which spanned the Cretaceous-Tertiary boundary. They could well be responsible for this mass extinction itself and the period immediately afterwards, when life was generally slow to recover. Significantly, the greatest number of last known occurrences of species in the fossil record coincides with the maximum frequency of these eruptions. The timing of these eruptions also corresponds with the date of the Chicxulub impact crater on the Yucatan Peninsula. Might there have been a "double whammy"?

There is no clear right or wrong in the debate about what happened to the dinosaurs. The curious thing is that not all animals or plants were wiped out. Freshwater species (such as crocodiles and frogs) survived, as did the birds and small mammals. Ferns suddenly diversified. It is a mystery that is unlikely to be solved soon.

An erupting volcano spews molten lava into the surrounding countryside. It eventually cools and solidifies.

Earth shook

Around 251 million years ago, almost all life on Earth became extinct. It was the greatest catastrophe in Earth's history. Most marine species were eradicated, including the trilobites, many coral species, and heavily armoured fish. Eight orders of insects (including many giant species) became extinct, and two-thirds of all species of terrestrial amphibians, reptiles, and mammal-like reptiles disappeared. It became known as the "Great Dying".

Like all mass extinction events, what happened is still a mystery. Impact from an extraterrestrial body (such as an asteroid), volcanic activity, sea-level changes, increased desert conditions, and a sudden influx of methane gas have all been blamed at one time or another. Catherine Powers and David Bottjer at the University of Southern California, USA, recently proposed a believable theory that combines elements of several of these traditional explanations.

Deep-sea die-off

The California team revealed that organisms in the deep sea were the first to die-off. These were followed by creatures living on reefs and in the shallow waters around continents. Finally, the last to go were animals on the shore. Whatever killed them must have originated deep down in the sea. They suggest that the most likely candidate is the gas hydrogen sulphide.

Prior to the mass extinction, it is thought that enormous volcanic eruptions occurred across the world, especially in Siberia where they are known as the **Siberian Traps**. The volcanoes released huge quantities of carbon dioxide and methane into the atmosphere. These gases caused a greenhouse effect

Dimetrodon was a mammal-like reptile that was a casualty of the Permian mass extinction. Its sail was probably used to regulate body temperature.

Dunkleosteus was a monster prehistoric fish approaching 10 m (33 ft.) long. It had razor-sharp bony plates instead of teeth, a heavily armoured head, and a body without scales. It died out, along with all its "placoderm" relatives, at the end of the Permian, about 251 million years ago.

that resulted in significant global warming. The warming oceans began to lose their oxygen and hydrogen sulphide, produced by bacteria in the deep sea, spread up to the surface and into the atmosphere. This gas damaged the ozone layer, so that harmful ultraviolet radiation reached the Earth's surface. The result of this was that about 90–95 percent of marine species and 70 percent of land species were killed off.

The same pattern of dying is also seen 199.6 million years ago at the end of the Triassic, when the Atlantic Ocean was beginning to form. Massive volcanic activity on the ocean floor, and the subsequent release of greenhouse gases, led to another period of global warming. The evidence indicates that volcanic activity was evident in all five major mass extinction events.

GREENHOUSE EFFECT

The greenhouse effect is the rise in temperature that the world experiences when certain gases in the atmosphere (such as carbon dioxide, methane, and water vapour) trap energy from the Sun. It is a natural phenomenon, and plays an essential part in keeping our planet warm. Without it the global temperature would be 33°C (60°F) colder. However, from time to time throughout Earth's history an overproduction of greenhouse gases has caused the global temperature to soar, even to the extent of melting the polar ice caps. Today, scientists believe human activities are producing greenhouse gases that are contributing to a global rise in temperature.

The largest trilobite so far discovered is 72 cm (28 in.) long. It lived 445 million years ago on an ancient tropical coast. It can be seen at the Manitoba Museum, Canada.

Ordovician and Devonian extinctions

During the Ordovician period, about 488.3–443.7 million years ago, Earth enjoyed long, warm, stable conditions. Multicellular organisms lived mainly in the shallow seas around and within continents. The biggest animal of the time was a giant **cephalopod**. With a long conical shell (known as an orthocone) and tentacles at one end, it was 11 m (36 ft.) long. It ate fish and giant sea scorpions, which themselves grew up to 2 m (6.6 ft.) long. There were also giant trilobites 72 cm (28 in.) long (see above).

About 444 million years ago all this changed. A hundred families of marine creatures disappeared, including the orthocones. The brachiopods, bryozoans, trilobites, conodonts, echinoderms, corals, and graptolites were hit particularly hard. These extinctions coincided with an exceptionally long ice age that came about when the southern supercontinent **Gondwana** drifted over the South Pole.

The cold **glacial** periods were interspersed with warmer periods. These changes caused the level of the oceans to rise and fall by more than 50 m (165 ft.). In the cold periods, seas within continents vanished and continental shelves were exposed, so the number of habitats was reduced. The cooler waters caused many species to die, and toxic substances drifted up from the bottom of the ocean to increase the death rate. During each cold period several species disappeared, until 85 percent of all marine species had gone. When the glaciers melted and stable conditions returned, the survivors diversified to fill all the vacant spaces left by the animals that went extinct.

March of the plants

During the late Devonian period, 416–359.2 million years ago, a mass extinction event known as the late "Devonian Crisis" took place. It occurred over a period of 20–25 million years, during which time there were eight to ten individual extinction events. Up to 80 percent of all animal species became extinct, especially those in shallow tropical seas, such as many coral species. Cold water creatures in temperate seas were unharmed. On land, *Archaeopteris*, the world's first tree and a relative of today's conifers, disappeared.

Before the crisis period, these land plants had been doing rather well. The evolution of seeds had enabled them to spread rapidly across the globe. Their roots broke up rocks, which lead to greater soil formation and weathering. This led Thomas Algeo of the University of Cincinnati, USA, to suggest a novel theory. Algeo noticed that the increase in vegetation on land, especially the newly evolving trees during the mid to late Devonian, resulted in more plant material being washed into the sea. The increase in nutrients in the sea led to algae, decay, and a reduction of oxygen levels in the water. This is called **eutrophication** and it killed many species. The same processes can be seen today in the Baltic Sea, where some parts are completely dead.

At the same time, there was less carbon dioxide in the atmosphere. This initiated global cooling and at the end of the Devonian it triggered an ice age, the last nail in the coffin. The newly evolved trees had been the agents of all this mass destruction, and the biggest culprit, *Archaeopteris,* was the architect of its own demise.

A "bloom" of algae, seen from the air, clogs coastal waters, removing oxygen so that few other organisms can survive.

HUMANS AND EXTINCTION

Five hundred years ago, the dodo was very much alive on the island of Mauritius. It was discovered in 1507. Some 180 years later, due to rats and cats brought ashore by visiting sailors, it was wiped out. This pattern was to repeat itself time and time again. There are many examples of human activity having driven plant and animal species to extinction.

The present geological epoch started about 11,430 years ago, towards the end of the last ice age and the start of the **Mesolithic** stone age in human culture. It also marks the start of a period in Earth's history when humans have caused other organisms on the planet to die out. It is considered by many scientists to be the sixth great mass extinction and is known as the **Holocene** extinction event.

The dodo was a flightless pigeon that stood about 1 m (3.3ft.) tall.

100 BC
Syrian elephant extinct in Middle East.

AD 1000
Moa-nalo, goose-like ducks, extinct on Hawaii.

C. 1500
Moa extinct in New Zealand.

Megalania was a giant monitor lizard that was even bigger than the modern Komodo dragon. It lived in Australia and preyed on giant wombats and other large marsupials. It became extinct about 40,000 years ago. Today, its closest living relative is Australia's perentie monitor lizard.

Lost species

Many of the species that became extinct during the past 15,000 years were large animals. On islands in the Mediterranean, the 2 m (6.6 ft.) giant swan of Malta was taller than dwarf elephants. In North America, the giant short-faced bear, standing 1.5 m (5 ft.) tall at the shoulder was the largest bear ever to have lived. It shared the continent with the dire wolf, the world's largest wolf, and a 2.5 m (8.2 ft.) long giant beaver. South America was home to giant ground sloths that reached a height of 6 m (20 ft.) when standing on their rear legs. In Australia, wombats the size of modern hippos and a giant kangaroo twice the size of today's red kangaroo were stalked by *Megalania*, a giant monitor lizard over 5 m (16.5 ft.) long.

In more recent times, the aurochs, a large species of wild cattle, died out in Europe. The last specimen was a female that died in the Jaktorów Forest, Poland, in 1627. The last tarpan, a species of wild horse, died in the Ukraine in 1918. In Australia, the last thylacine, or Tasmanian tiger, died in a zoo in 1936. Steller's sea cow, a giant **manatee** that inhabited the Northwest Pacific, was discovered in 1741 and was extinct by 1768, a period of less than 30 years.

C. 1680
Last auroch dies.

C. 1681
Last dodo on Mauritius.

1768
Steller's sea cow extinct in North Pacific.

1884
Great auk extinct in North Atlantic.

1914
Last passenger pigeon dies in North America.

| 1600 | | 1750 | | 1900 | Present day |

Who or what killed the North American megafauna?

Mammoths and mastodons, along with camels, llamas, and wild horses once roamed North America. They were part of the North American megafauna, meaning "large animals". Following them closely were lions, cheetahs, and sabre-toothed cats, including *Smilodon*. *Smilodon* was a specialist. Its bite was less powerful than a lion's but it could open its mouth 120° (compared to the lion's 65°). Its enormous canine teeth were used to slash the throat of young mammoths. Any threat to the mammoths would mean trouble for *Smilodon*.

Around 12,800 years ago, mammoths and other large herbivores in North America went extinct, and so *Smilodon* died out as well. A classic case of co-extinction – but why did they go?

Three theories

1. Paul Martin at the University of Arizona, USA, suggests the herbivores were hunted to extinction. At about the same time that mammoths went into decline, the Clovis people arrived from Asia. They spread across North America and Martin believes that wherever they went they killed all the large herbivores, including mammoths.

A supernova is an exploding star that appears extremely bright. It radiates more energy in a few weeks than the Sun produces in 10 billion years, driving a shock wave at a tenth of the speed of light (which is 299,792,458 metres per second) across its part of the universe!

RADIOCARBON LEVELS IN ICELANDIC SEDIMENTS

▼ The three peaks in these radiocarbon levels indicate events caused by a supernova explosion. The last event coincides with the extinction of mammoths in North America.

2. Donald Grayson at the University of Washington, USA, argues that climate change was to blame. At the end of the Ice Age, the mix of woodland and grassland in North America gave way to extensive grasslands with different grass species. Hot, dry summers were followed by icy cold winters. For half of the year North America dried out, and during the other half food was buried in deep snow. The mammoths died out because they could not cope with these extremes of temperature.

3. Ross D. E. Macphee at the American Museum of Natural History, New York, put forward the notion that a changing climate caused the mammoth's range to shrink at the time people arrived. However, he feels that it was disease rather than hunting that led to its final extinction. He believes viruses brought by people or their animals, such as dogs, killed off North America's big game.

Supernova

A similar megafauna was thriving in Eurasia at this time, so whatever the cause, it affected North America alone. Richard Firestone at the Lawrence Berkeley National Laboratory, USA, believes debris from a **supernova** 250 light years away hit North America 13,000 years ago. An impact layer, high in radioactivity, is present at Clovis hunting sites where human activity ceased at the same time mammoths disappeared. Firestone points out that two shock waves would have preceded the debris, one at the time of the explosion 41,000 years ago, followed by a second one 34,000 years ago. Significantly, 34,000-year-old mammoth tusks have been found peppered with iron-rich grains that must have hit at a speed of 12,000 km/sec (7,500 miles/sec). Firestone believes the supernova debris, that followed some time later, eliminated the mammoths.

Unbelievable loss

It is hard to believe that passenger pigeons once filled the skies of North America. In the early 19th century it was probably the most numerous bird species on the planet. Flocks of over 2,000 million birds were over 1 km (0.6 miles) wide and 500 km (300 miles) long. They were so dense that it was said they blotted out the Sun. In their nesting sites, trees came crashing to the ground under the weight of birds! The passenger pigeon was undoubtedly one of the most successful animals on Earth. Not for long.

The pigeon provided cheap meat. By 1860, full time pigeon hunters were capturing up to 2,000 birds at a time in huge nets. During one hunt in Michigan in 1878, 1,000

"STOOL PIGEONS"

Passenger pigeons were lured to their death by putting out live birds as decoys. The decoys were nailed by their feet to a post and had their eyes sewn shut. Their desperate fluttering enticed other birds down to take a look. These were the original "stool pigeons" – dummy pigeons.

million birds were killed. By 1896, only 250,000 birds were left at Bowling Green, Ohio. In 1900, a boy in Pike County, Ohio, shot the last wild bird. In the Cincinnati Zoo in 1914, "Martha", the only bird in captivity, died. Human hunters had achieved what many believed impossible. In just five decades one of the most common animals on Earth had become extinct.

It is estimated that 5 billion passenger pigeons lived in North America before the European settlers arrived. They nested communally with a hundred or more nests in a tree.

COMMITTEE ON RECENTLY EXTINCT ORGANISMS (CREO)

CREO is based at the American Museum of Natural History, New York. Its stated role is "to foster an improved understanding of species' extinctions that have occurred in recent times". In this case, "recent" refers to extinctions that have occurred since AD 1500 (when natural history records became more reliable). Scientists from all over the world contribute to CREO. They work on surveys of extinct species so that we can better understand why and how animals become extinct.

On their books is the golden toad of Costa Rica. This bright orange toad, no more than 5 cm (2 in.) long, was discovered in cloud forests in 1966. By 1989 it had been declared extinct. The toad probably died from a fungal disease that is attacking amphibians all over the world. Scientists at the Monteverde Cloud Forest Preserve have discovered the situation has been made worse by global warming. Night-time temperatures in the cloud forests have risen, but increased cloud cover has led to cooler days, making conditions ideal for the fungus. It kills amphibians by stopping them from absorbing water through their skin. This suggests that amphibians are in the first wave of extinctions caused by global warming.

▶ *The golden toad is just one of 20 amphibian species that have disappeared from a 30 sq. km (11 sq. mile) study area in the Monteverde cloud forests of Costa Rica. The only place to see the toad now is in the archives of wildlife filmmakers.*

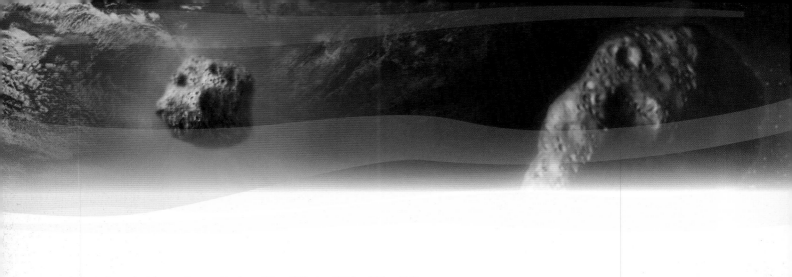

HEADING FOR
EXTINCTION

Extinction rates today, based on known extinctions during the past 100 years, are estimated to be 50–500 times higher than average. The current **Holocene** extinction is thought to be 10–100 times greater than any mass extinction event of the past. The World Conservation Union (see page 34) has documented 785 known extinctions since AD1500. There are a further 68 species found only in captivity and therefore extinct in the wild. In the past, most extinctions have been on islands in the oceans. Today, just as many species are disappearing from the continents. About 50 percent of extinctions during the past 20 years have been on continental landmasses, and this only accounts for known animals. Most species living on Earth have yet to be discovered, such as the many living in tropical rainforests or the ocean depths. This means unknown numbers of organisms are probably going extinct before we even know they are there at all. Estimates vary, but some calculations suggest that Earth might be losing species at a rate of 140,000 per year!

1918
Carolina parakeet extinct in USA.

1936
Tasmanian tiger extinct in Australia.

C. 1952
Caribbean monk seal last seen in USA.

The Mekong catfish is critically endangered due to overfishing, loss of water quality, and river dams. Its numbers have declined by 80 percent in the last 15 years.

Animals at risk

Animal extinction isn't evenly spread. About 21 percent of amphibians are critically endangered or endangered. About 10 percent of mammals and 5 percent of bird species are endangered. Fish are poorly documented. It is not known how many are threatened, but 18 percent of known shark and ray species are endangered.

Where those at risk live

Most threatened species live in the tropics. Countries with tropical islands have the highest number of threatened species. Many threatened marine mammals are in the North Pacific, eastern Indian Ocean, and southwest Pacific.

Causes of extinction

Causes of extinction include natural changes in an animal's living space, as well as human activity. Habitat destruction (such as deforestation) is the main threat to all animal groups. **Alien species** have a great impact upon birds living on islands. Amphibians are particularly hit by pollution, including global warming and disease. In the seas, overfishing is currently hitting fish stocks hard. Fisheries that use long fishing lines with many hooks also kill seabirds, such as albatrosses. The birds try to steal the bait from the hooks and are caught. They are then dragged below the surface and drown.

1989
Golden toad extinct in Costa Rica.

1994
Saint Croix racer snake extinct in US Virgin Islands.

1997
Aldabra banded snail extinct on Indian Ocean island.

2000
Last Pyrenean ibex died when a tree fell on it.

2007
Woolly-stalked begonia extinct in Malaysia.

RED LIST

The Red List of the International Union for the Conservation of Nature (IUCN) is the most complete inventory of the world's most threatened species. It was created in 1963 in order to assess extinction risk. Each species is evaluated at least once every five years and the list is updated annually. Species are placed in one of 10 categories based on:

- rate of decline;
- population size;
- geographic distribution;
- fragmentation of populations.

The IUCN applies the term "threatened" to endangered, critically endangered, and vulnerable species. In the latest update, the western lowland gorilla was regraded from "endangered" to "critically endangered". This is due to habitat destruction, poaching, and vulnerability to the Ebola virus. The Yangtze river dolphin is listed as "critically endangered (possibly extinct)", making it the most endangered **cetacean** in the world. The entire habitat of the woolly-stalked begonia in Malaysia was cleared for farming. Searches for the plant in neighbouring forests have revealed nothing for 200 years. This plant has now been officially declared extinct.

Recovering species

Most species on the Red List get moved from a less threatened to a more threatened category. However, there are a few species that improve their position on the list through conservation programmes or because new information becomes available. The Mauritius parakeet has been removed from the "critically endangered" list, due to successful conservation measures, and is now classified as being "endangered". As new information becomes available some species are reassessed and a few are put into a less serious category. The Madagascan pochard was thought to be extinct, but a small population of 13 birds was rediscovered in 2006, and it is now "critically endangered".

RED LIST CATEGORIES

Category	Code	Example
Extinct	EX	Dodo
Extinct in the wild	EW	Barbary lion
Critically endangered	CR	Sumatran orang-utan
Vulnerable	VU	Gaur
Lower risk/ conservation dependent	LR/cd	Springbok
Near threatened	NT	Leafy sea dragon
Least concerned	LC	Norwegian rat
Data deficient	DD	Thresher shark
Not evaluated	NE	Humans

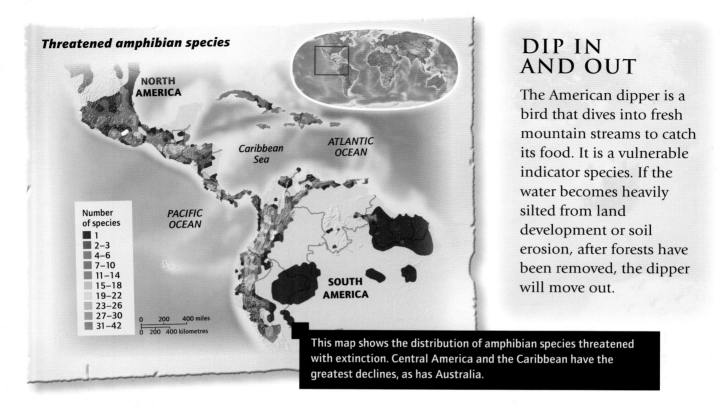

Threatened amphibian species

NORTH AMERICA

Caribbean Sea

ATLANTIC OCEAN

PACIFIC OCEAN

SOUTH AMERICA

Number of species
- 1
- 2–3
- 4–6
- 7–10
- 11–14
- 15–18
- 19–22
- 23–26
- 27–30
- 31–42

0   200   400 miles
0 200 400 kilometres

This map shows the distribution of amphibian species threatened with extinction. Central America and the Caribbean have the greatest declines, as has Australia.

DIP IN AND OUT

The American dipper is a bird that dives into fresh mountain streams to catch its food. It is a vulnerable indicator species. If the water becomes heavily silted from land development or soil erosion, after forests have been removed, the dipper will move out.

Indicator species

Indicator species are animals in the wild that give an early warning if something is wrong with the ecosystem. The problem they highlight could be disease, pollution, climate change, or invasion by an introduced species. Indicator species are those most sensitive to a particular change to their environment and most likely to be the first to go extinct if the change worsens. Lichens (algae and fungi living together) are especially sensitive to air pollution, particularly sulphur dioxide – a pollutant from car exhausts and industrial fumes. If air quality is good, lichens grow in abundance; if it is poor, they die off.

Frog warning

Amphibians are especially useful indicators of environmental change. They absorb chemicals through their skin so react to pollution in water or air. Of more than 6,000 known species of amphibians, about a third are threatened. They may have been on the planet for 300 million years, but during the past few decades species have been disappearing rapidly. About 170 have already become extinct and populations of a further 2,500 known species are in decline. The frogs are telling us that something is wrong.

Harlequin frogs of South and Central America are endangered because of fungal disease triggered by global warming. About 67 percent of the species have disappeared in recent years.

Rainforest is slashed and burned at an alarming rate. This means that the world's largest pharmacy is disappearing and with it the medicines that could fight human diseases.

Rainforests, biodiversity, and extinction

The International Union for Conservation of Nature (IUCN) estimates that 99 percent of all the threatened species on Earth are at risk from human activity, with the most threatened habitat being the tropical rainforest. The equivalent of 20–50 soccer pitches of forest disappears every minute. At one time, 12 percent of the Earth's surface was covered with rainforest. Today, that figure is closer to 5 percent. It is cut down for timber and to make way for cattle and crops, but untold numbers of plants and animals are removed, too. The rainforest is home to the greatest number of species of plants and animals on Earth, most of which are still to be discovered. By removing rainforests the planet's **biodiversity** is being reduced.

Lungs of the world

Rainforests store carbon and release oxygen, and so help to control the balance of oxygen and carbon dioxide in the Earth's atmosphere. They also have an important role in the maintenance of the world's climate. Rainforests receive more rain than any habitat on Earth. Rainforest zones, such as the Amazon and Congo basins, not only have their own **microclimates**, but also influence the weather elsewhere. So much energy is released in tropical rainstorms that it influences atmospheric circulation across the entire planet!

Natural pharmacy

Not only the trees disappear when rainforests are cut down. Rainforests are filled with potential new foods to feed the starving and drugs to combat serious diseases. Roughly 80 percent of our foods originated in rainforests, but of the 3,000 known fruits, today we only consume about 200. Around 25 percent of modern medicines were also discovered in the rainforest. Recent research has shown that over 3,000 rainforest plants have anti-cancer properties. An extract from one plant, the rosy periwinkle from Madagascar, has been used successfully to treat childhood **leukaemia**. When people clear the rainforest they are destroying medicines of the future.

RAINFOREST PLANTS AND THEIR USES

Plant	Use	Geographical origin
Rosy periwinkle (*Catharanthus roseus*)	Vincristine – treats childhood leukaemia	Madagascar
Curare tree (*Strychnos toxifera*)	Curare – muscle relaxant	South America
Cinchona tree bark (*Cinchona spp.*)	Quinine – malaria cure, painkiller with anti-inflammatory properties	South America
Wild yams (*Dioscorea spp.*)	Diasgenin in contraceptives	North America and India
Kombé seeds (*Strophanthus spp.*)	Ouabain – heart stimulant	Africa
Golden trumpet (*Allamanda cathartica*)	Flowers – laxative	South America
Annatto or lipstick tree (*Bixa orellano*)	Colouring in cheese, rice, and lipstick – also protects against UV (ultraviolet)	South America
Pineapple (*Ananas comosus*)	Food, also contains bromelain that has anti-inflammatory properties	South America
Peach palm (*Bactris gasipaes*)	Food with more oils, carbohydrates, and protein than maize	South America
Rubber tree (*Hevea brasiliensis*)	Natural rubber – many uses, from car tyres to rubber gloves	South America
Cebu cinnamon (*Cinnamomum cebuense*)	Oils for perfume and pharmaceutical industries	Philippines
Patchouli (*Pogostemon cablin*)	Perfumes and natural insect repellent	Asia
Honduras rosewood (*Dalbergia stevensonii*)	Musical instruments	Central America
Black pepper (*Piper nigram*)	Spice and seasoning	Southern India
Vanilla orchid (*Vanilla planifolia*)	Flavouring in foods	Central America
Fragrant nutmeg (*Myristica fragrans*)	Spice	Southeast Asia and Australia
Cassava (*Manihot esculenta*)	Tapioca pudding – also a staple food in some developing countries	South America
Calameae (*Calamus spp. and others*)	Rattan furniture	Indonesia
Green ramie or rhea (*Boehmeria nivea*)	Textiles	Malay Peninsula

Death of the seas

It was long felt that people could have little impact on something as vast as the world's oceans. They cover 71 percent of the Earth's surface, yet even here the effects of human activity are being felt. Large areas of the Baltic Sea in northern Europe are completely dead, due to algae removing vital oxygen. North Atlantic stocks of cod have almost been fished out, and tuna have nearly disappeared from the Mediterranean Sea. Seafood throughout the world is contaminated with heavy metals from industry, such as mercury. Plastic shopping bags kill marine life when animals swallow them, thinking they are food. In the Arctic, polar bears and other marine mammals have very high levels of dangerous chemicals in their bodies.

Marine biodiversity hotspots

Tropical coral reefs are especially vulnerable. Like the rainforests on land, coral reefs are biodiversity hotspots under the sea. In recent years, a quarter of tropical reefs have been destroyed along with the organisms that live there. They grow slowly, between an inch and a couple of feet each year. Australia's Great Barrier Reef is the largest in the world and may have taken five million years to build. **Coral polyps** build the reefs, but growing inside them are algae (zooxanthellae). The algae get shelter and nutrients from the food caught by the tiny polyps. The polyps receive additional food via **photosynthesis** in the algae. For this, the algae need sunlight so tropical corals grow in warm, shallow seas. The complex and delicately balanced coral reef ecosystem

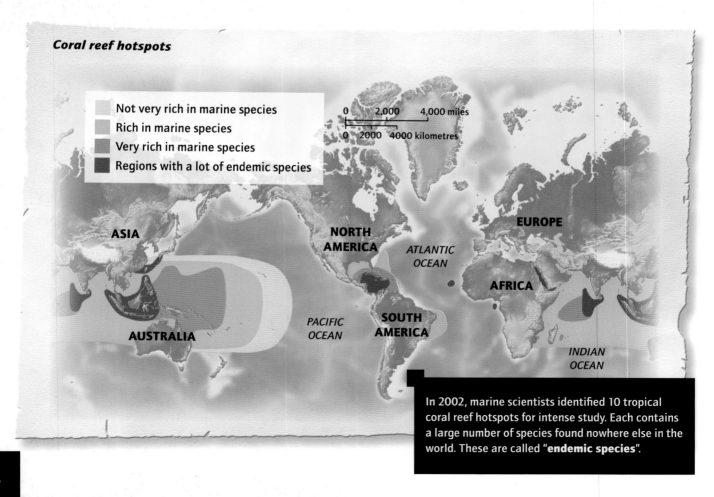

Coral reef hotspots

Not very rich in marine species
Rich in marine species
Very rich in marine species
Regions with a lot of endemic species

0   2,000   4,000 miles
0   2000   4000 kilometres

ASIA

NORTH AMERICA

ATLANTIC OCEAN

EUROPE

AFRICA

PACIFIC OCEAN

SOUTH AMERICA

AUSTRALIA

INDIAN OCEAN

In 2002, marine scientists identified 10 tropical coral reef hotspots for intense study. Each contains a large number of species found nowhere else in the world. These are called **"endemic species"**.

is the basis of a **food web** involving about a quarter of all sea life. Up to 2 million species benefit from a single reef, all of which are threatened with extinction.

Hotspots threatened

There are many threats to coral reefs. When trees in tropical rainforests are removed, silt and soil is washed into rivers and carried to the sea where it can clog tropical reefs. The use of dynamite to catch fish damages hard corals, and cyanide used to catch fish for the aquarium trade kills more fish than are taken alive. Coral mining for tourists also destroys large areas of reef. The main concern is coral bleaching caused by global warming. At higher temperatures, the zooxanthellae inside the polyps move out. If conditions do not change the polyps die. About 10 percent of tropical reefs have already degraded beyond the point of recovery.

REEF EXTINCTIONS

The fate of corals and coral reefs has been well documented in the fossil record. Corals have not always been the primary reef-building organisms. Recognizable coral reefs date back to 195 million years ago, but fossil reef structures are found in rocks 450 million years old. Certain species of blue-green algae, sponges, and polychaete worms are reef builders. One 350 m (1,148 ft.) long reef was built on a Welsh beach by honeycomb worms in just two years. In addition, Earth has recovered from many episodes of widespread reef extinctions. The threat to coral reefs today is not new. Somehow, they always seem to bounce back – though this time, they may need a little help.

Corals can be delicate like this sea fan (above), robust like brain and pillar corals, or branching like staghorn corals. Whatever their size and shape, they are vulnerable to change, especially to the warming of the sea, when they die (below).

OVERCOMING
EXTINCTION

Extinction may be inevitable, but in some circumstances it can be delayed. There are several different ways to save a species from dying out. Some methods require patience and dedication, others use advanced technology.

Captive breeding

One way to rebuild a population and save it from extinction is to breed rare or endangered species in captivity (in zoos or wildlife parks). If the wild habitat recovers, or the original threat to the species is removed or reduced, the captive-bred animals can then be reintroduced. However, this is not straightforward. If the species is close to extinction, the population and its **gene pool** are too small for it to remain healthy. This could lead to problems with inbreeding. In a healthy, wild population there is a great diversity of genes so if a fatal disease hits, some are likely to survive. As all animals in an **inbred** population have similar genes, they are less likely to have immunity. A single disease could then lead to extinction.

Operation Oryx

In order to save a species, it must be realised it is in danger before it is too late. In 1972, the last wild Arabian oryx was shot dead. But since

1975
White-tailed eagle reintroduced to Britain.

1980
Brush-tailed bettong reintroduced to the wild on Australia's St Francis Island.

1982
Arabian oryx reintroduced to the Arabian Peninsula.

1984
Golden lion tamarins reintroduced to Brazil's Atlantic Coast forests.

| 1975 | 1980 | 1985 |

SUCCESSFUL CAPTIVE BREEDING AND REINTRODUCTIONS WORLDWIDE

Species	Principle captive breeding/release agency	Reintroduction to
Black-footed ferret	Wyoming Fish and Game Department, USA	USA/Mexico
California condor	San Diego Wild Animal Park/Los Angeles Zoo, USA	USA/Mexico
Musk ox	United States Fish and Wildlife Service	Alaska
Pere David's deer	Woburn Abbey, UK	China
Nene or Hawaiian goose	Wildfowl and Wetlands Trust, UK	Hawaii
Pink pigeon	Durrell Wildlife Conservation Trust, Jersey, UK	Mauritius
Przewalski's horse	Foundation for the Preservation and Protection of Przewalski's Horse, Netherlands	Mongolia
Lammergeier	Vienna Breeding Unit, Haringsee, Vienna	European Alps
Brush-tailed bettong	Australian Wildlife Conservancy	South and West Australia
White-tailed eagle	Royal Society for the Protection of Birds, UK	Western Scotland
Golden lion tamarin	A group of world zoos coordinated by the GLT Conservation Program	Brazil
Partula snail	Durrell Wildlife Conservation Trust, Jersey, UK and a number of zoos, including Detroit Zoo, USA	French Polynesia

1962, London's Flora and Fauna Preservation Society had organised for animals in private collections to take part in a **captive breeding** program. In 1982, Operation Oryx saw the reintroduction of zoo-reared animals to the Arabian Peninsula. Phoenix Zoo in Arizona had been at the centre of the initiative. They sent animals to other zoos until enough were reared to send into the wild. Populations are now increasing in Saudi Arabia, Israel, and the United Arab Emirates. Due to poaching and severe habitat loss, the population of oryx released in Oman is falling.

A carefully co-ordinated captive breeding programme, initiated by the Fauna and Flora Preservation Society of London, UK, brought the Arabian oryx back from the brink of extinction.

1986
Lammergeier reintroduced to the European Alps.

1987
Mauritius kestrel reintroduced by Durrell Wildlife Conservation Trust.

1995
Wolves reintroduced to Yellowstone National Park, Wyoming.

2002
Reintroduced California condors breed for the first time in the wild.

| 1990 | 1995 | 2000 |

Frail fry

Scientists have found that steelhead trout, when bred in captivity, are less likely to survive in the wild than wild-born fry (baby trout). **Genetic mutations** build up in the captive population, as in any population. However, because the captive population is not subjected to **natural selection** in the same way wild populations are, some of the mutations can be harmful. A study at Oregon State University, USA, showed that 40 percent of baby steelhead trout from captive-bred parents are less likely to survive to adulthood. So captive breeding is not the answer to saving all wild animal populations.

Cloning mammoths and the *Jurassic Park* syndrome

Michael Crichton's fictional book, *Jurassic Park*, saw dinosaurs brought back to life by duplicating biological material – a process known as cloning. In the story, John Hammond's scientists took damaged dinosaur DNA from the gut of a 100 million-year-old mosquito trapped in amber (fossilised resin from trees). The damaged DNA was spliced with DNA from modern reptiles and birds. It was then put into a modern reptile egg from which the **nucleus** (therefore, the DNA) had been removed. The egg hatched and grew into the creature matching the new genetic information – a dinosaur.

Crichton's idea would have remained just a story had it not been for the cloning of **Dolly the sheep**, at Scotland's Roslin Institute, in 1996. This success led scientists in Russia and Japan to try cloning a mammoth. They tried extracting DNA from the remains of frozen mammoths, buried in Siberia's permafrost, to place in an Asian elephant egg (its closest living relative). But collecting the DNA has proved more difficult than anybody would have guessed. So for the moment this mammoth dream remains just that – a dream.

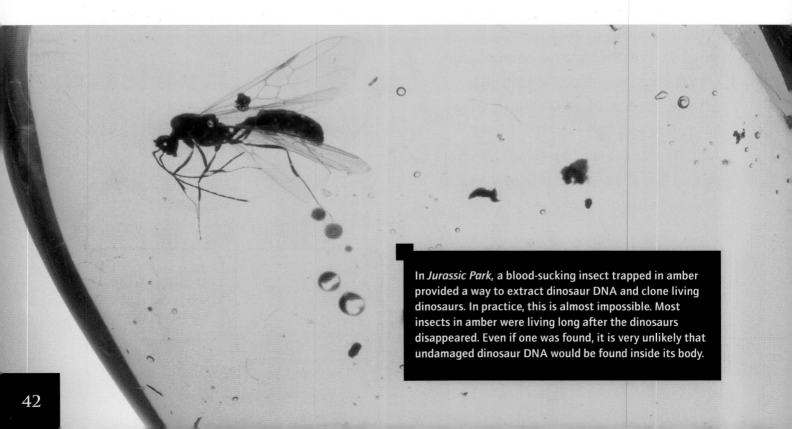

In *Jurassic Park*, a blood-sucking insect trapped in amber provided a way to extract dinosaur DNA and clone living dinosaurs. In practice, this is almost impossible. Most insects in amber were living long after the dinosaurs disappeared. Even if one was found, it is very unlikely that undamaged dinosaur DNA would be found inside its body.

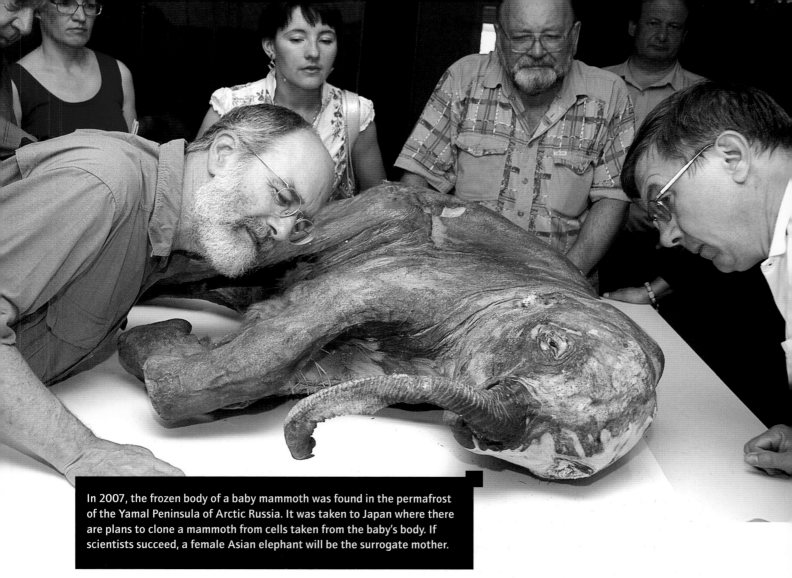

In 2007, the frozen body of a baby mammoth was found in the permafrost of the Yamal Peninsula of Arctic Russia. It was taken to Japan where there are plans to clone a mammoth from cells taken from the baby's body. If scientists succeed, a female Asian elephant will be the surrogate mother.

Cloning endangered species

Conservationists have adopted the technique of cloning with limited success. The mouflon, a species of wild mountain sheep from Eurasia, was cloned in 2001 at the University of Teramo, Italy. It was the first endangered animal to be cloned successfully. Mouflon DNA was placed in the egg cells of domestic sheep in a similar way to that in which Dolly the sheep was cloned.

The banteng, a wild ox that was once common in southeast Asia but whose numbers have dwindled, was cloned in 2003 using the eggs of domestic cattle at San Diego's Centre for Research on Endangered Species. In the future, scientists are hoping to clone tigers, giant pandas, mountain gorillas and other rare or endangered species.

Cloning, however, is unlikely to help the Iberian ibex, which once lived in the Pyrenees. The last surviving Iberian ibex lived in Spain's Ordesa National park but in 2000 a tree fell and killed it. Tissue samples were taken with the hope of cloning it, but all the clones would be female so the Iberian ibex will not have a chance to breed naturally in the wild. That is unless, of course, scientists find a way to splice in male genes from its closest living relative.

A scientist removes samples of frozen viruses that had been immersed in liquid nitrogen at a temperature of -196°C (-320°F). The same technique can preserve genetic material from endangered species.

Gene banks, seed banks, and the "Frozen Zoo"

Gene banks can be used to preserve genetic material, providing insurance in case a species becomes extinct. Plants can be preserved as frozen cuttings or as seeds. Animals can be preserved as **embryos**, eggs, sperm, tissues, blood, or DNA samples.

Two of the most wide-ranging gene banks are found in the USA: the Zoological Society of San Diego's "Frozen Zoo", and the National Audubon Center for Research of Endangered Species, Louisiana. San Diego's "Frozen Zoo" keeps material from over 800 species or **subspecies**. The National Audubon Center keeps a frozen bank of over 1000 species. including the gorilla, the Sumatran tiger, and the mountain bongo (a type of antelope).

Animal tissues are kept in vials that are immersed and frozen in liquid nitrogen at the staggeringly cold temperature of -196°C (-320°F). In theory, the tissues can be thawed if needed and used to recreate animals that have long been extinct. It is thought the material can be frozen in this way for thousands of years without it deteriorating.

At the Louisiana facility, an African wildcat was created by fertilising an egg in the laboratory. This process is known as "in vitro fertilisation". The embryo was frozen then later defrosted and implanted in the uterus of a domestic cat. This process is known as **interspecies embryo transfer**. The result was an African wildcat kitten named Jazz. Jazz was cloned twice to create two identical

These African wildcats were bred in captivity using cloning techniques. Ditteaux (left) is a clone of Jazz (right). Ditteaux went on to be a natural father to several more generations of captive-bred wildcats, proving that cloned individuals can breed naturally and contribute to the preservation of the species.

wildcats named Ditteaux and Miles. It was one of the first successes using **cryogenics** (low temperature technology), and a first step in reversing the process of extinction.

WILDCATS

The African wildcat is one of a group of small cats that includes the domestic cat. The African subspecies lives throughout Africa, except in the rainforests. It is protected in some countries but not all. The greatest threat to the species is breeding with domestic or feral cats, which would mean that the offspring would not be purebred wildcats.

Rare grass

In 2007, a British scientist working at Belgium's National Botanic Garden found some grass seeds deep in a vault. All that remained of the species were these 3,000 seeds. Some of the seeds were planted locally, but only a quarter of them germinated. So the other seeds were sent to the Millennium Seed Bank at the Royal Botanic Gardens in Kew, London. Here, the grass seeds grew. The grass turned out to be that of a species last seen in an area of Belgium and France about 70 years ago.

THOUGHT TO BE EXTINCT BUT REDISCOVERED

Species	Last seen	Rediscovered
Woolly flying squirrel	Late 19th century, Pakistan	1990, Pakistan
Gilbert's potoroo	19th century, Western Australia	1994, Western Australia
Canterbury knobbed weevil	1922, Christchurch area, New Zealand	2004, Burkes Pass, New Zealand
Ivory-billed woodpecker	1944, Singer Tract, Louisiana, USA	2004, Big Woods area, Arkansas, USA
Southern takahé	1898, South Island, New Zealand	1948, Lake Te Anau, New Zealand
Bermuda petrel or cahow	1620, Bermuda	1951, Castle Harbour Islands, Bermuda

Hidden away

Sometimes extinction is not forever; or rather the Red List (see page 34) designation of extinction is not. There are some plants and animals declared extinct in recent times that have been known to turn up many years after they were declared extinct. These animals tend to be ones that are small or camouflaged, and have as a result gone unnoticed despite scientists' best efforts to find them.

For instance, it was the unusual call of a green tree frog, high in a tree in Costa Rica, that attracted the attention of British researcher Andy Gray, from Manchester Museum. It transpired that he had rediscovered a creature thought to have been extinct for 20 years. Similarly, the Bavarian pine vole, the Lord Howe Island stick insect, and the New Zealand storm petrel have also "returned from the dead".

The storm petrel was thought to have gone extinct when three were shot on New Zealand's South Island in 1850. But, in 2003, ornithologists spotted the species near the Mercury Islands, off New Zealand's North Island. The vastness of the Pacific and the obscurity of breeding burrows on remote islands probably accounted for the lack of sightings.

In the plant kingdom, nobody had seen the small pink flowers of Mount Diablo buckwheat, on its California mountain, since 1935. Therefore, the plant was thought to be extinct. However, in 2005, young botanist Michael Park, from the University of California at Berkeley, USA, could not believe his eyes when he came across a patch of early blooming Mount Diablo buckwheat. Seeds were collected and a rescue propagation programme activated. Even so, the plant is

The delicate pink flowers of Mount Diablo buckwheat were thought to have been lost forever, until a botany student chanced upon a plant. Since then, seeds have been taken to the University of California Botanical Garden, USA, for propagation.

still critically endangered and the site is kept a secret in case overzealous visitors should trample it.

Unfortunately, the vast majority of entries in IUCN's Red List are unlikely to have such a second chance. Most species on the list are heading inexorably to the brink of extinction. The human brain has more than 100 billion neurons and a thousand times more connections between them. Unless some of that amazing computing power is used to address what many scientists believe to be the "sixth mass extinction", the world is going to be a much poorer place.

TIMELINE

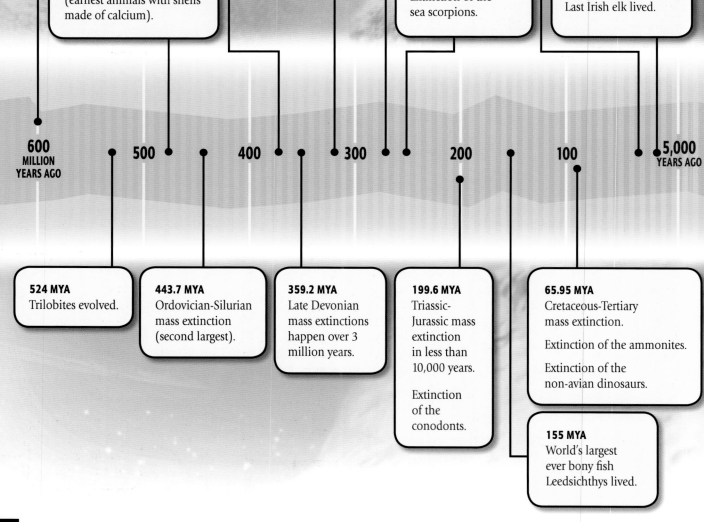

600–542 MYA
New period, the Ediacaran, when multicellular life forms populated the Earth, recognised by the International Commission of Stratigraphy.

385 MYA
World's earliest trees, such as the tree fern-like Wattieza and the modern tree-like Archaeopteris, evolved.

270 MYA
Ginkgo or maidenhair tree, similar to those found today, lived.

23 MYA
Fossil teeth similar to those of living frilled shark.

488.3 MYA
Cambrian-Ordovician mass extinction.

Extinction of the cloudinids (earliest animals with shells made of calcium).

318 MYA
Extinction of the graptolites.

251 MYA
Permian-Triassic mass extinction or the "Great Dying" (largest known).

Extinction of the trilobites.

Extinction of the sea scorpions.

15,000 YEARS AGO
Start of the Pleistocene mass extinction event.

12,800 YEARS AGO
Sabre-toothed cat *Smilodon* went extinct.

7,700 YEARS AGO
Last Irish elk lived.

600
MILLION
YEARS AGO

500

400

300

200

100

5,000
YEARS AGO

524 MYA
Trilobites evolved.

443.7 MYA
Ordovician-Silurian mass extinction (second largest).

359.2 MYA
Late Devonian mass extinctions happen over 3 million years.

199.6 MYA
Triassic-Jurassic mass extinction in less than 10,000 years.

Extinction of the conodonts.

65.95 MYA
Cretaceous-Tertiary mass extinction.

Extinction of the ammonites.

Extinction of the non-avian dinosaurs.

155 MYA
World's largest ever bony fish Leedsichthys lived.

TIMELINE CONTINUES ON PAGE 50

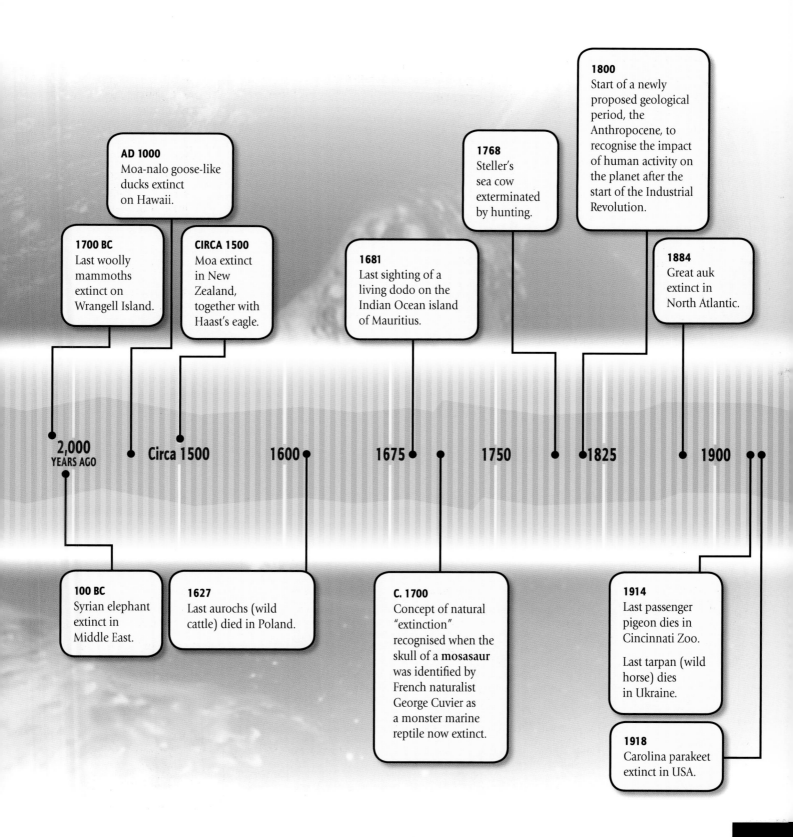

AD 1000
Moa-nalo goose-like ducks extinct on Hawaii.

1700 BC
Last woolly mammoths extinct on Wrangell Island.

CIRCA 1500
Moa extinct in New Zealand, together with Haast's eagle.

1681
Last sighting of a living dodo on the Indian Ocean island of Mauritius.

1768
Steller's sea cow exterminated by hunting.

1800
Start of a newly proposed geological period, the Anthropocene, to recognise the impact of human activity on the planet after the start of the Industrial Revolution.

1884
Great auk extinct in North Atlantic.

2,000 YEARS AGO   **Circa 1500**   **1600**   **1675**   **1750**   **1825**   **1900**

100 BC
Syrian elephant extinct in Middle East.

1627
Last aurochs (wild cattle) died in Poland.

C. 1700
Concept of natural "extinction" recognised when the skull of a **mosasaur** was identified by French naturalist George Cuvier as a monster marine reptile now extinct.

1914
Last passenger pigeon dies in Cincinnati Zoo.

Last tarpan (wild horse) dies in Ukraine.

1918
Carolina parakeet extinct in USA.

TIMELINE CONTINUED

1936
Last known Tasmanian tiger dies in Hobart Zoo.

1938
Coelacanth found to be alive and well and living off South Africa and Comoro Islands, although thought to be dead 70 million years ago.

1975
White-tailed eagle reintroduced to Britain.

1969
US palaeontologist John H. Ostrom identifies similarities between dinosaurs and birds.

1990-1999
Brush-tailed bettong reintroduced to mainland South Australia after trials on islands.

Laotian rock rat found in market, but species thought to have been dead for 11 million years.

Saint Croix racer snake extinct in US Virgin Islands.

Wolves reintroduced to Yellowstone National Park, Wyoming.

Dolly the sheep cloned in Scotland.

Aldabra banded snail extinct on Indian Ocean island.

African wildcat, Jazz, born to domestic cat after interspecies embryo transfer.

2006-2007
Long-legged Gracilidris ants rediscovered although thought to have become extinct 15 million years ago.

Madagascan pochard rediscovered after having been classified as extinct.

Yangtze river dolphin is listed as "critically endangered (possibly extinct)", making it the most endangered cetacean in the world.

Woolly-stalked begonia extinct in Malaysia.

| 1950 | 1960 | 1970 | 1980 | 1990 | 2000 | **PRESENT DAY** |

PRESENT DAY
Holocene extinction

1951
Bermudan petrel rediscovered – considered extinct since 1620.

1952
Caribbean monk seal last seen.

1982-1989
Arabian oryx reintroduced to the Arabian Peninsula.

Golden lion tamarins reintroduced to Brazil's Atlantic Coast forests.

US palaeontologist Jacques A. Gauthier, Yale University drew a cladogram that grouped the birds firmly with dinosaurs.

Lammergeier reintroduced to the European Alps.

Mauritius kestrel reintroduced by Durrell Wildlife Conservation Trust.

Golden toad of Costa Rica declared extinct.

2000-2005
Last Pyrenean ibex dies when tree falls on it.

Mouflon cloned in Italy.

Reintroduced California condors breed for the first time in the wild.

Benteng (wild ox) cloned in USA.

Ivory-billed woodpecker rediscovered – thought to be extinct since 1944.

Mount Diablo buckwheat rediscovered in California after they were thought to be extinct since 1935.

FIND OUT MORE

Further reading

And Then There Was One: The Mysteries of Extinction, Margery Facklam and Sierra Club Books (Little, Brown, 1993)

On the Brink of Extinction: The California Condor, Caroline Arnold and Michael Wallace (Gulliver Green, 1993)

The Extinction of the Dinosaurs, Don Nardo (KidHaven Press, 2004)

General reference sites

The following websites will take you further into the subject of evolution and extinctions.

University of California Museum of Palaeontology
http://www.ucmp.berkeley.edu/index.php

University of California at Berkeley
http://evolution.berkeley.edu/evolibrary/home.php

London's Natural History Museum
http://www.nhm.ac.uk/

New York's American Museum of Natural History
http://www.amnh.org/

Smithsonian Institution
http://www.si.edu/

Chicago's The Field Museum
http://www.fieldmuseum.org/

Biology news

News of new developments in life sciences can be found at:
http://news.bbc.co.uk/2/hi/science/nature/
http://www.sciencedaily.com/
http://sciencenow.sciencemag.org/
http://www.newscientist.com/news.ns

Topics to research

Find out more about the "Big Five" mass extinction events.
Which animals went extinct and when?
Try watching: *Asteroids: Deadly Impact* (National Geographic Video, 2003)

Find out more about the "Frozen Zoo" and other similar facilities.
What animals are they saving from extinction?
Try looking at:
http://cres.sandiegozoo.org/index.html

http://agsrca.srivilasa.com/frozen_zoo.htm
http://www.cincyzoo.org/
http://www.auduboninstitute.org/site/
PageServer

Find out more about cloning mammoths.
Where are frozen mammoths found?
Try reading:
Mammoths and Mastodons, Susan Heinrichs Gray, (Child's World, 2005)
Outside and Inside Woolly Mammoths, Sandra Markle (Walker & Company, 2007)

Find out more about "living fossils" and "Lazarus species".
Look up living fossil plants, such as the dawn redwood, horsetails and the ginkgo. See if you can track down pictures of the living plants and the fossils that look similar to them. Why is the giant panda sometimes considered a living fossil? What are the hoatzin, tuatara, and pearly nautilus?

Read about the remarkable story of the discovery of the coelacanth in:
Old Fourlegs: the Story of the Coelacanth, J. L. B. Smith (Longmans, 1956)
or the updated account in:
A Fish Caught in Time, Samantha Weinberg (Fourth Estate, 1999)

Find out more about the large blue butterfly and its relationship with a red ant.
Do other butterfly species have similar links with ants or other insects?

Find out more about global warming, climate change and its impact on wildlife.
Take a look at the following websites for more information:
http://www.noaa.gov/
http://royalsociety.org/
http://www.epa.gov/climatechange/

Check out the IUCN Red List.
See which species are on it at:
http://www.iucnredlist.org/

Do some botanical research.
What kind of research work is carried out at the Royal Botanic Gardens at Kew, London?
Take a look at:
http://www.kew.org/
Look for the world's other botanic gardens.

Discover tropical foods and medicines.
Make a list of all the foods that originally came from a tropical rainforest. Then make a list of medicines that had their origins in tropical rainforests. Do medicines come from other wild places, such as coral reefs or temperate woodlands?

GLOSSARY

adaptive radiation a process by which several species evolve from a single parent species, each one being specifically adapted to survive in a different environment

aerosols fine dust or liquid droplets in a gas, which can come from volcanoes and aerosol spray cans

algae large group of simple plant-like organisms that are able to photosynthesize but do not have leaves and vascular tissue

alien species organisms living outside their normal range that have invaded and adversely affected other ecosystems (also known as "invasive species")

ammonite extinct group of marine molluscs, related to octopus, squid and cuttlefish (cephalopods), which outwardly resemble the living pearly nautilus

amphibians vertebrate animals with four legs that live part of their life in water, and the females of which produce eggs that have no protective shells

background extinction the general rate of extinction between mass extinctions

biodiversity variation of life forms in an ecosystem, biome or on the entire Earth

Cambrian a major division or period in the geological timescale that began about 542 million years ago and ended 488.3 million years ago

captive breeding rearing of endangered wild plants and animals in zoos and parks with the view to releasing them in the wild places from which they originally came

cephalopods major group of molluscs that have a prominent head together with arms or tentacles, such as squid, octopuses, cuttlefish, and ammonites

cetaceans whales and dolphins

cloudinids early multicellular family of animals, consisting of calcium tubes, that died out at the start of the Cambrian

coelacanth ancient lobe-finned fish, thought to be extinct at the end of the Cretaceous but found alive and well in the seas off South Africa, Madagascar, and the Indonesian island of Sulawesi

co-extinction when two organisms die out because one depended on the other

conodonts extinct eel-like marine animals resembling miniature lampreys or hagfish

coral polyp the living part of a coral which resembles a small sea anemone

Cretaceous a major division or period of the geological timescale that began about 145.5 million years ago and ended 65.95 million years ago

cryogenics study of very low temperatures

definitive host the host in which a parasite reproduces sexually

Devonian a major division or period of the geological timescale that began about 416 million years ago and ended 359.2 million years ago

DNA stands for deoxyribonucleic acid, which contains all the genetic instructions for the development and functioning of a living thing

Dolly the sheep the first animal to be cloned from an adult body cell by the process of nuclear transfer

embryo the earliest stage of development from the moment the fertilized egg first divides to the moment of hatching or birth. In humans, it refers to the first eight weeks after fertilization; thereafter it is called a fetus.

endemic species organisms that live exclusively in one part of the world

Eocene a major division or epoch of the geological timescale that began about 55.8 million years ago and ended 33.9 million years ago

eutrophication increase in chemical nutrients in an ecosystem that causes excessive growth of organisms, such as plants and algae. This results in poor oxygen levels and a severe reduction in water quality to the detriment of many animals and other plants.

fauna animals from a specific region, habitat, or time

food web the feeding relationships between species

gamma rays a form of high-energy radiation or light emission that has shorter wavelengths than X-rays. They kill living organisms. Gamma rays are produced when stars collide or explode and could be responsible for mass extinctions on Earth.

genes units of inheritance that are an organism's instruction manual. Genes determine how an organism looks and the way it works.

gene bank means of preserving genetic material from plants or animals

gene pool complete set of unique characteristics of a species or population

genetic diversity the total number of genetic characteristics in the genetic makeup of a species

genetic mutations changes to the sequences of genes of an organism

glacial relating to processes and landforms caused by glaciers

Gondwana southern supercontinent that existed 500–200 million years ago, which included all the landmasses in the southern hemisphere today

graptolites major group of colonial animals that lived from 510–320 million years ago

Holocene a major division or epoch of the geological timescale that began 11,430 years ago and continues until the present day

inbred breeding between close relatives of plants or animals, which results in a lack of genetic variation

intermediate host a host in which a parasite does not reproduce sexually but may grow or reproduce asexually

interspecies embryo transfer the insertion of viable embryos of one species into the female of another species

interstellar matter the gas and dust between star systems within a galaxy

iridium a chemical element that was found in large quantities in clays laid down at the end of the Cretaceous, when the dinosaurs disappeared. The layer could have been the result of the Earth's collision with a large extraterrestrial body or from volcanic eruptions.

Lazarus species organisms that have disappeared from the fossil record only to reappear again later

leukaemia cancer of the blood or bone marrow

light year distance travelled by a beam of light in one year, approximately 9.46 million million kilometres (5.88 million million miles).

manatee a plant-eating marine and freshwater mammal that lives on the coast and in rivers along the Atlantic coasts of South and Central America and West Africa

maniraptoran a group or clade of dinosaurs that includes the birds and the dinosaurs that were closely related to them

Mesolithic "middle stone age" from the end of the Ice Age to the start of farming

microclimate a local atmosphere zone where the conditions differ from the surrounding area, such as under a log

Miocene a major division or epoch of the geological timescale that began about 23.03 million years ago and ended 5.33 million years ago

mosasaurs group of powerful serpent-like marine reptiles that lived at the time of the dinosaurs but were actually lepidosaurs with overlapping scales

myxomatosis a disease that infects rabbits

natural selection the process by which favourable inherited characteristics become more common and less favourable ones become less common in successive generations

nucleus a membrane-enclosed organelle found in cells, which contains the cell's genetic material

Oort comet cloud a spherical cloud of comets that are located a thousand times the distance between the Sun and Pluto from our solar system

Ordovician a major division or period of the geological timescale that began about 488.3 million years ago and ended 443.7 million years ago

ozone layer a layer in the Earth's atmosphere that contains high concentrations of ozone. It absorbs 99 percent of the Sun's high frequency ultraviolet rays that could damage life on Earth.

parasite an organism that lives on or inside another organism and causes it harm

Permian a major division or period of the geological timescale that began about 299 million years ago and ended 251 million years ago

Phanerozoic an overall division or eon of the geological timescale that began 542 million years ago, when the first hard-shelled animals appeared, and continues today

photosynthesis the conversion of light energy from sunlight into chemical energy using carbon dioxide and water

plankton tiny organisms that inhabit the sea or freshwater

Pliocene a major division or epoch of the geological timescale that began about 5.33 million years ago and ended 2.59 million years ago

predator an organism that consumes other organisms

pseudo-extinction occurs when no more individuals of a species survive, but members of a daughter species remain alive

Siberian Traps a vast area of ancient lava floes, the result of the largest volcanic eruption in Earth's history. The activity coincided with the Permian-Triassic mass extinction event.

Silurian a major division or period of the geological timescale that began about 443.7 million years ago and ended 416 million years ago

solar wind a stream of particles that are ejected from the upper layers of the Sun's atmosphere and prevented from reaching Earth's surface by its protective magnetic field

subspecies a classification term that is ranked below "species". It refers to a group of animals that are not distinct from the species from which they originate. They may have been separated from their ancestors by mountains or seas, but have not yet become a distinct species.

supernova an exploding star, which for a brief time appears extremely bright

Tertiary a major division or period of the geological timescale. It began with the demise of the dinosaurs 65.95 million years ago and ended at the start of the most recent Ice Age 2.59 million years ago. It includes the Pliocene, Miocene, Oligocene, Eocene, and Paleocene epochs.

Triassic a major division or period of the geological timescale that began about 251 million years ago and ended 199.6 million years ago

trilobites extinct arthropods that resemble modern woodlice but are not directly related to them. They appeared in the Cambrian period. The last species of trilobite disappeared during the Permian-Triassic mass extinction event.

ultraviolet radiation radiation with a wavelength shorter than visible light but longer than X-rays. It is part of the radiation from the sun, and is painfully evident when it causes sunburn.

vertebrate an animal with a backbone

INDEX